RIVERBOOK & OCEAN

Riverbook
& Ocean

W. H. New

OOLICHAN BOOKS
LANTZVILLE, BRITISH COLUMBIA, CANADA
2002

National Library of Canada Cataloguing in Publication Data

New, W. H. (William Herbert), 1938-
    Riverbook & ocean

    Poems.
    ISBN 0-88982-208-5

    I. Title.
PS8577.E776R58 2002   C811'.54   C2002-910103-4
PR9199.3.N395R58 2002

The Canada Council | Le Conseil des Arts
for the Arts | du Canada

We gratefully acknowledge the support of the Canada Council for the Arts for our publishing program.

BRITISH
COLUMBIA
ARTS COUNCIL
Supported by the Province of British Columbia

Grateful acknowledgement is also made to the BC Ministry of Tourism, Small Business and Culture for their financial support.

We acknowledge the financial support of the Government of Canada through the Book Publishing Industry Development Program for our publishing activities.

Published by
Oolichan Books
P.O. Box 10, Lantzville
British Columbia, Canada
V0R 2H0

Printed in Canada

For Peggy

Acknowledgments

This book owes much to many friends: Charles Dawson, whose elegant river-writing spurred me to write these poems; Laurie Ricou and Jack Hodgins, who read early drafts of the manuscript and offered helpful suggestions; Ron Smith, Hiro Boga, and Jay Connolly at Oolichan Books, whose support and guidance has been constant and invaluable. "Undertow" appeared earlier in "The Pirates in the Looking-Glass," an essay I contributed to *Small Worlds*, ed Rocío G. Davis and Rosalía Baena (Pamplona: Ediciones Universidad de Navarra, 2001).

CONTENTS

I. Riverbook & Ocean

II. Shorelines

III. Garden Bed

IV. Taking Turns

I. Riverbook & Ocean

l. Riverbook & Ocean

1. PREOCCUPATION

A single figure on the lakeshore
turns mesmerized—haunted by silence,
the lap of shadow—twists
away from the water and back again,
drawn by rival designs:
shimmer, & paralyzing cold.

The light looks strong enough
to step on, the shiver grips
the back of the neck, reptilian,
clamps its teeth on guilt
& old shame, tarnished
twins of revelation.

Who is the watcher here
who stands, undivided,
undercover in shades?
Monitor. Monitor. Trained
to read the fugitive pause
at the liquid lip of choosing.

2. DIVISION

All know the scissor-man,
   see the rock he stands on,
      mid-rapids, through
      spate's haze, the border blur
      of imperfection, & yet

most, rescinding reason,
   call upon impression's twist
      to navigate the river:

they learn only slowly
   time's recursive:
      turns upon itself
        as hungry dogs snap
        jaw-wise at the pack,
      slices,
      severs repetition,
      tumbles *again* in difference,
      spins eddies over stone.

3. Impression

What decided him, old painter,
canvas caked in clay white,
to make manganese grow
irises at pond's edge,
what shaped his mind's wilderness,
gardened waterworld into seen field,
blurred borderline till all that mattered
was intensity: light,
light, and more light, sudden
recognition, spring's desire,
disappearance in the far reaches
of blue—
          Before the brush touches
leaf, the mind's eye's convinced
it sees life entire, pressed
in iridescence, colour rapid,
escaping into river running, sky.

4. Vanishing

They huddle by the watercooler
whispering *O*—
                or *No*—
                            intake,
out-take, converting mouth and brow
to disbelief and shock, the public
lineaments of loss.

                        Thirty years
earlier, they'd have shared
secrets in lemon juice, squirrelled
paper slips in pockets, blank
till afterschool reopened them
warm with messages. *O.*
No. Rearranging eager into
wave:

        the secret gone the moment
of its telling, love & numbered love
both fired into whisper as words
fade from the page—again, again:
the codes buried deep in body-
memory, tongued as corporate desire.

5. Reopening

You see it in the papers, not
every day, but often enough
it comes to seem unremarkable,
some county sheriff in West
Virginia's pressed to exhume a body,
dredge a river, drain a pool—
suspicious circumstances—there's
the phrase, and passive—*have been drawn
to the attention of*—& maybe
then a name, & on to the next
item.
      For some it means more:
(the father who wants rough justice,
the neighbour who always suspected, the grey
lizard in the shadow who lusts after carrion,
decay).

      You never see the other stories, though,
the ones where life goes on:
Boy picks scab in park,
Storekeeper opens door at 9,
Old man refuses to recollect his youth.

6. ATTENTION

How attention wanders, drifts
    canyonwards, rafts white
    water out of breath & into
    shoal, shore, surprise: crests
    the next wave & the next, then
    skips abruptly into open
    air, sails over alpine
    tundra, animals as stunned as carbor-
    undum at the scentless moth gliding
    past them into revelation . . .

lurches back to algebra,
the alphabetic stand of certainties,
the scramble for equation on the valley floor:

binomial to the finish, mindful of what's
left after undertow and number.

7. UNDERTOW

No doubt it seemed simple:
the young coach treats his team
of ten-year-olds to a day at Spanish
Banks: he doesn't plan the rip-
tide, doesn't intend danger,
or heroics, just a game
called Sunday afternoon.

The 3 o'clock turn still whips
four boys suddenly out to sea.

One plot runs like this:
hero saves youngsters, KISS
OF LIFE ON SUMMER FORESHORE—
Another rumbles counter-point: FOOL-
HARDY ACTION WASTES YOUNG LIVES.

Neither floats free. *What
If* shivers off Point
Grey, under wraps, like ice
drawn in   onto headland.

8. Foreshore

At dead low tide the sand
stretches nearly to Point Atkinson
Light, and yet, reaching the dark
water, edge of shoal, the child
sees there's still room for seven
freighters to lie at anchor—even
more—others ply silently,
toys at sea, off the horizon.

*

Partway to shore, where the sand
undulates in nibbled ridges
& tiny crabs clutch the stranded
pools, another child, or another,
squats with pail and tin spade,
plans lapsed castles, digs
moats to Queensland, draws lines
against the unimaginable deep.

*

Is that himself he sees, sunhat
askew, from the lawn chair in the chicory?
And is that also him, oblivious
to atlas-makers, tussling
friendship, trailing soccer shoes,
walking arm-in-arm with the moon?
Yes. Here. Blanketed
in summer, lost in crenellations.

9. FRIENDSHIP

Yes, there are friends along the way,
you know who you are,
this is for you: it belongs to you
because you do not have to see it
to know what it says, it says love,
trust, pleasure, joy, a pressed
rose, a dog-eared photograph
of caught laughter, soft rain—

if you imagine these words,
run, rose, photograph,
listen for the pealing playground,
shouts, whispers, the ripple of talk
all magnified in silence,
knowing silence is not loss,
just these words, the telling
sound of riverbook and ocean.

10. MAGNIFICATION

Where is it, we ask; they answer *under glass*, anticipating awe:

under glass: space kept aside,
available to ordinary
life, but held apart, thunder
without the lightning, blunder
without blood, like open secrets
in a house of mirrors: *under glass*:

> 1. the place of old photographs,
> grandfather with his eyes glazed
> in cataracts, father in collar
> and wide tie, mother looking
> down, away from the sun:
> > 2. the place
> of fuchsias over winter, seed
> packets, green geraniums, wonder
> without worry:
> > 3. the place of odd
> ornaments, porcelain-headed
> pheasant with blue tear, rainbow
> molecule, large as life
> on a petri dish, magnificent
> as promise: *under glass*:

but be wary: even
the ordinary breaks: *look
but don't touch*: the print grows
small, the mirror dim, we need
a longer telescope to see:

sunder, loss, without losing.

11. Reflection

```
M I R R O R O R
R O R R I M M R
O R O R O R I I
R R O R O R R M
R I R ? R I R M
I M R I M M O I
M M I R R O R R
M I R R O R O R
```

12. PERIMETER

QED, he said, a half-
smile crossing his face, though what
he proved eluded us as often
as it brightened him. Euclid.

Daily we walked diameters
outside his classroom walls, raised
perpendiculars, traced
ratios of time & motion without
thinking of Pythagoras.

                        Now
they've all gone, and looking back,
those few of us remaining shamble
through the terms we memorized
(cone, compass, square), ragged,
never having learned the complex
shape, the plain perimeter
of *pi.*
            Now, even the half-light
might appease.

                        At sea, we wish
the old masters grace, Cartesian
fields to march in, balancing
equations as they go.
                        For them
the lines were real, at least *seemed*
real, and they believed—they *said*
that they believed—in logic.

                              Not
for us. When we crossed gamely
into what we thought was open space,
we lost the ease of order:
                              lines
numbers   flap like torn sails,

and proof's a patched scarecrow, grown
grey with sunrise, soluble
as creekside, elusive as a chalked
circle's end. *QED.*

13. GAME

Upstream, some rivers
go underground, disappear
in stock options, bog or dry
bed, Alexis Creek running
cattle, Alice Springs just
dust & gumtrees, schooners
& flies; but every year at Alice
brawny men race the Todd
barefoot, haul their boats hip-
high along the parched channel,
fully loaded, loser buys
the beer, *No worries, mate.*

At Anaheim, stream and swamp
alive with midges, trout, salmon
roe, you'd think *fecundity*,
osprey diving, bear and cougar
lapping at the brink.
                    The grizzly count's
down though, and everywhere
fingerlings die of toxic
spill, spawning grounds spoil:
the rook's already changed
perches, & the kingfisher's vulnerable.

At Alice, in the wet, they drink
indoors, ignore the thunder pummeling
the metal roof. At Riske Creek
the river's milk, at Dog Creek
and Big Bar already muddy.
Prophets wander in vain looking
for the corrugated desert:
summer's held in check by deerflies,
rifle, campervan, and hail.

14. DISAPPEARANCE

Posters everywhere depict
loss—persons missing from
house and home,
                  blonde toddler
            gone from picnic into thin
     air; under-age pro-
          stitute, last seen in plaid
            jumper & black eye shadow;
    Alzheimer's patient shuffling
         in pastel nightshift
    deeper & deeper into the dark—

they come back rarely, mostly
disturbing sleep, head-&-shoulder
nightmares snatched from the family scrapbook,
shaping line   by absence
*lacuna, hole, hollow, puncture,
hernia,*
        word unsaid, posterity

river stolen from the green place,
dammed by deferral, by delay.

15. PATIENCE

The stepsister tells the Mouse to move it—
black jack onto red queen,
she wants knockout flash and instant
resolution WIN or GAME OVER

> *over there, next to the picture*
> *of Mary cradling Christ, Cinderella*
> *plays solitaire slowly, by the fire,*
> *hands caressing each card*

Cardinal virtue/ cardiac arrest:
in the palace it's always either/
or: the algebra of choice
meaning no choice, finally

> *finally playing the perfect game,*
> *finding the numbers, colours flow*
> *in sequences of revelation,*
> *the tactile joy of close contact*

Contact eludes them both, that's why
they play, their busyness screens
screaming at the old lady's glass,
the prince's broom, the time of day

> *Daylight spools forward into*
> *others' lives, leaves them with midnight*
> *mice, holding thistle bouquets,*
> *shredding paper on the parquet steps*

16. Sequence

The third brother crossing the bridge
always gets the troll, not
the first or second: they're too busy
with brawn and ego: he's the one
who unravels riddles, and lives,
for unclear reasons, longer.

You can see him now, standing tall
in centre span, counting *one-
two-three* but not jumping,
not yet, mumbling *later*
after next then   working
his way towards *therefore*, the logic

he thinks, of readiness. Unlikely.
Below him the river *he* sees
races in separate raindrops, each
in sequence. It's not the maelstrom pausing him,
but the brown gap between *now*
and *late*, when the bone river's dry.

He cannot leap, the third brother:
even knowing the river's rain,
ocean, tributary, flow, he listens
only for evaporation, stands
with trolls, only stones below them,
all lined up and nowhere to go.

17. SEPARATION

Master mariner—George Vancouver aboard the longboat—
misses in fogbank the Great River's mouth
dividing, the roil of red sockeye & oolichans rising.
Netted in regulation, he maps on through sheer
sounding, fathoming only the white wall of distance.

> Upstream, tributaries mimic the delta,
> withdraw like tendrils into private space,
> clinging at life, marsh ooze & protozoa,
> creating, re-creating rush in the muck & muscle
> of watercycle: life massing all around him

but George rows north into ice-wind,
oblivious. His oarsmen pull him away, while the tide favours,
prepare to part while still he dreams of flying, before
he changes his mind again, orders *Discovery*'s sheets
hauled in, & trades duty for blind compulsion.

18. Privacy

Poverty on skid road
grants a kind of privacy:
the man urinating off
the sidewalk, the muffled blanket
cries, others know but do not
see or hear,
                    while hedged lives
in Rosedale are bought & eaten
daily in the tabloids,
advertised, digested, spat
out
                    everyone wanting touch
& working for distance, wanting a place
a/part   where they'll be *in* at last,
& working not to want, or want to need.

```
    A
    P
A  PART    APART
    R
    T
```

The paradox of ligature:
distance joins, joining sep-
arates, like random
coupling on Wreck
Beach, Bondi, Noosa Heads

hunger at a table set for one.

19. PURCHASE

Barnacles & mussel clusters catch the pilings, grip
in & out of tidewater twice a day
while streams of seaweed drift leeward, windward,

salt pendulum suspended from the moon.
The wharf is alive, the generations walking its length
& back scarcely aware of tumult underneath—

old couples with canes and field glasses step
slowly, search the distance for steamships & memory;
young couples swim each other's bodies; girls,

boys, with lines and wormtins, hook shiners
onto the creosoted planking, calling *Mum!*
Dad! Come see! and they do, moments for all

they could not buy, buried by day's end like
geoducks & castles under the captivating
ripples of the chased sand, the warm & lethal sea.

20. Suspension

Breathing in, the kayakers flip over
in the rapids, regain air scarcely noticing
the cables overhead, the tremulant hanging bridge,
the seven tourists on it—six bubbling *Oh,*
Oh, Oh, preparing their faces till later, when
they can write postcards, say *Fabulous*
Just fabulous—haven't stopped shaking!—

and six of the seven don't see them, or know
they later get home safe, or care, or notice
the one who does, the one who is watching the water,
wondering whether to leap   *maybe climb*
next time past the safety rail, slip
accidentally into upside-down, embrace
the whitewater's hold in the unrelenting green.

21. Safety

Icarus as a boy played with army
trucks, not frisbees, played cops-&-
robbers, marbles in a ring, not hop-
scotch, kites, addy-addy-I-
over: he watched the ground, held fast
to things—water, earth—turning away
from dangerous fire & insubstantial air.

You'd have forecast for him an ordinary job—
something that kept his hands occupied,
farm irrigation, yard work in the maze,
something that gave him the lie of the land. But he held
fast because of the gnawing away: it was always
there, & the first leap up he was vulnerable—
monster on one side, father on the other,

alternating tales of damnation &
derring-do—inexorably, flame drew him,
& air appeared to hold him up: what
the old stories never tell is whether
he regretted choosing, or lived finally
only at the point of falling, knowing at last the difference
between fear and safety, tumbling into the sea.

22. SEA

The earth gives way at the sea's edge:
invisible, toxins sluice from mill-site
& dumping-ground out into salt,
defer, defer:

             At the sea's edge
        a poster cautions NO BEACH
        FIRES   NO VANDALISM
        NO IMPROPER BEHAVIOUR.
                        A smaller
        sign, hand-written, warns
        of plankton blooming, red tide,
        feeding the pink macomas, heart
        cockles, littlenecks, horse
        & butter clams with silent poisons
        that trial by fire cannot kill,
        nor cold nor overseas.

                        A blue
heron stands on sandstone, preening,
eyes alert for food and present danger.

23. HANDWRITING

Lightfoot strumming the railway, Rogers
reading Franklin's poisoned scrawl—
they dream passage, sing destiny
& destination, places to stand
complete. The Other Side. Pacific.
Beaufort Sea. *mene mene*
tekel
            the handwriting's obscure,
set down in haste, the reading
certain only of the need to read—

Is it the singers, or songs themselves
that re-enact the *voyageurs,*
strike tocsins at Ste-Anne's, the setting
out tolled slowly as though
not belonging were suspect, syn-
onymous with cardinal desire.

They are not lost, those who follow
distance across the watershed,
the spell of current, cursive dream,
but one with the marvellous:

                singing, they range
Northwest, melody their *grand
portage,* carrying all who listen
with them out of the ice, along
the canyon walls, writing the world
anew in riverbed and motion.

24. SYNONYMS

And yet every heart dreams its own November—
sings by sunshine, falls asleep in the poppy fields,
Dorothy, Dorothy, dropping out of time, exhausted
by repetition and despair: are they monsters,
those who snare, or just another face of love,
the spur to rise again, *walk on, walk*
on, walk on . . .
               The soldier at the cenotaph
is 86, tottering now, but still wearing her ribbons
boldly, halting into memory as she lays the wreath
with a youngster's help, wandering again to the canvas ward,
the chloroform, the pain of phantom limbs she couldn't
ever quite subdue . . .
               What is it they say,
about the same river? Sometimes, despite the current,
a single pool invites the diver back, longing,
looking for bones in distance, desire: a dark time
before the whirlwind, or during, when arms embraced, legs
moved, and dream & loss did not yet coincide.

25. Ghosts

You see them everywhere, like faces
startled out of family photographs,
old uncles with bulbous eyes,
starched women fired by Temperance
& the politics of union—they peer
over hedges, out of the back
of clothes closets, up from under
leaf litter in shallow pools:
whispering   lost bodies, small
moth-words, unforgiving
actions clasped crabwise—they
murmur in the dark places, twist
torso till the four limbs hang
useless, flap like drunk banners
after rain—
                    in the quiet,
when water gliders stamp tantrums,
they coil *past past past*
on smoke-wings, till you forget
why you pay attention to the river,
its drift and run to sudden sea.

26. PROHIBITION

They start off saying
                    DON'T DROWN,
the beach signs: say
                    SLIP SLAP
SLOP, warning of treacherous currents, skin
cancer, the ozone holes, all framed
as institutional defences—
                              over
night, graffiti artists tell the world
they see it differently
                    ON   OWN
                    S   AP

The spray paint works wonders,
giving them blanks to live in, staving off
bitterness in irony. O zone.

            END   POLLUTION   NOW
            BAN   THE   BOMB

            END │ POLLUT │ NOW
            BAN │   E │ BOMB

But no. They cannot stop it, cannot stop it
happening again, again, cannot
stop the moment, cannot stop it, cannot

27. A Drowning

Imagining angels
        the man in the rubber black wetsuit
on the other side of beaded ice
        bobs in the Coral
the man standing
        swallows   strokes twice   falls
where sheer cliffside meets the sky
        under   calls
dreams the call
        HELP   *where next the rip leaves him*
HELP   watches through gauze   vapour
        swallows   strokes
helpless   held
        falls silent   apprehending
immobile in mid-element   vortex
        undertow
seeking meaning
        possibility   small hope   angels in
        helicopters
all air whirling   waving
        finding him   diving
in Queensland blue
        nearby to reach him   the safety
        ladder
life the merest ripple of desire
        swinging empty

in decision
>   *overhead   the man   disappearing*
an hour   two   merging
>   *under the surface*
fixed firmanents
>   *slurred   tossed   lost beyond*
first hopes   wings   regret
>   *recovery   blades*
breaking breath
>   *breaking   abating south   the body*
salt   crystal   coral   cold
>   *given up*
into sibilance
>   *at last   cased ghost walking*
rappelling into distance   unready
>   *given over*
already borne
>   *to white shark   curtain sea*

28. Breaking

air

    curves
there

light
    turns
        as though
nothing's
       changed

traces
    sand scallops

       ribs

frets
    soft
       rock
into
    blue
       furrows

air   pulses

    rakes

    lungs
full of
       sea

29. CURVE

The bend in time happens before the tale begins or
else the hero never notices he knows already already
how he's part of the world he wanders through
scattering time aside embracing day by dawn & here
by nightfall there by loss & every hour each slow ever
step returns him surfacing the long sine wave of sleep
giving way to breath again to breath again moving on
yes unready unready moving on

30. ALREADY

The prince in the riverbook has an ordinary job
cleaning up a small corner of the world
a pool here a backwater there
prying loose the jammed logs re-
cycling the tossed cans the aimless
glass maintaining space for the coho the spring

at night he goes home sings gently
Row Row Row Your Boat he does not
have a blue room does not fear midnight
does not lock away old distances—
No—he looks forward to the touch the over-
lap of day and darkness ripple of skin

dissolving boundarylines he does not under-
stand love or try to   knows only
ache in absence joy in return   round
the earth's imagined ice   tropic palm
& pebbled sand   rain and river shiver-
sea and rain   already one   embracing

II. Shorelines

II. Shorelines

WAVE

Tongues of iris &
   ocean
lick in tandem
air's edge &
   shore,
   touch
curved lip &
curved lip, skim
   there &
      brushing firm
   there,
curl away &
come again
        reaching
   ripple
   for the sun, ripple
reaching
   for the moon.

MAUI

Haleàkal'à's quiescent,
brooding red at the thousand
trails, the serpentine paths that
men & women carve to creep along.

In dream the rifts open,
vent steam & ash, land becomes river
running fire.

If you listen,
you can hear thunder building.

Or look, read the sea's mis-
directions: ocean
tugs at the shore, the currents,
jacaranda blue.

STRANDING

Beaches mark the edge of some named
and some nameless islands—sand littoral
for castle moats and coupling, long evening

walks in time with the waves—and mass landing
craft attacks, guns & arrows, cross-
beams planted on overlapping shores.

Other islands end in cliff, chalk
& stone abrupt as buckshot, height affording
cannonfire, clamber claiming vista.

Painters draft allegories out of both:
seaside eden (power in parentheses),
rude bluff (banked in the back room).

Gulleys mutter a different universe.
In channels dense with undergrowth, creeks
chatter clear & pebble-wise down

& down to where the edge is indistinct,
but talk & tide embracing even here
spell slowly into place a border.

CHOIR PRACTICE

Thursdays at 7 the ten or twelve
faithful volunteers gather
at the C of E to practise Sunday's
hymn, *You who unto Jesus,*
their voices waving gamely
at the Anthem & plainsong psalms.

Down the road, the Pentecostals
rock: electric hallelujahs
thump & twang, country-&-western
turned affirmative, *You
are my Harbour, Sail
my Boat,* the fellowship of ties.

If you listen, you can hear others,
urging the long withdrawal to end,
ritualists, still in love
with Latin, dreamers, doubters, mute
swans communing privately,
chanters, refusers, old crows.

Seagulls soar above the ferryboat,
pursuing food—   practise dart-
&-dive—   unstoppable as singing—
braid the air like six-part harmony,
as small streams lace a stony
channel into praise, into rage.

Aries, bound

The mountain goat does not know it follows
the same track it followed last year,
& generations earlier tramped into place.

So when was the first goat, the one who said
There, chose *that* rock to climb & not
another—leaping with such poise into emptiness?

Perhaps each age fosters its own
originals: earth itself liquefying
in fire & flood, submerging pattern, turning

land again only in the cool,
when delta flourishes where nothing was
but sea, & lava beds nurture algae,

lichen, moss, & step by step the pathways
of the ruminants—although the sea is
not nothing: barnacles build on sunken

wrecks, shaping underwater mountains,
& every reef was once bright coral,
living its birthplace into sustenance & shelter.

Where is the line, then, that separates *after*
from *before*? (In chaos.) Who draws it? (Chaos.)
And what is chaos? (Just the refusal, ready

or not, only to follow)—but wait: look:
is that design? those tree-tips, April
rain, waves on a rocky coast— or game?

LETTING GO

There
      and again
There
      and again
There
      and again
There

      and again
There

      and again

There
      and again

There

      and again

There

      and again and

*

Pacing between one wall and another
you learn the space you call accommodation—
roam, repeat, give way: no one attends,
leaving you the amplitude of absence
to wander in. Breath. Over the doorway hangs
a sampler saying ROSES INVENTED GARDENS
TO GROW BY but you're no longer sure: of that
or anything. Except the letting go.
Roses invented morning maybe, but all
day's laced with lattice, the fretwork shaping
cavities for afterwards to walk through,
embroidering the rooms with souvenirs
from there—wherever *there* is—ever's end.

REMAINDER

The *Buy-&-Sell* every week
advertises garage, garden
sales, some neutral, the practised
urging MUST MOVE, ESTATE
DISPOSAL, THREE-FAMILY-GROUP.

The folks who get interviewed
on talk shows swear they've found
antiques in back alleys, real
Leonardos in the jumble
on the white elephant table.

But is it jetsam or just flotsam,
drifting from harbour to grey
harbour like tramp steamers or the last
family to move off the block
to Out There, Somewhere New.

Leavings. Even the auctioneer
piles stuff left over
in the lumber room. *Mona,* for instance,
an early version, frowning at a shop
window. Knowing they'll be knocking
off a dollar next day.

GALIANO, SEPTEMBER AFTERNOON

The painter coaxes colour from the dry
croak of crows, strokes the hoarseness of the dun
grass into cadences of spice & longing.

Emily, the trees are yours, yellow cedars
filtering shade, holding their breath & moving,
red arbutus peeling patterns in the canopy,
firs chafing silently with chased cones.

Entering Active Pass, the Swartz Bay
ferry sounds its horn, the echo welling
over Bellhouse & Bluffs Park. The crickets ignore
the lowing wail. The white colt in the upper
pasture scarcely lifts its head. Only
the transients check their watches, murmur *The 3,*
The 5, tell themselves they've left time
on the Mainland somewhere, over there, waving
dumb at the uninterrupted sky.

BIRD LANDING

Moments before a crow lands,
its legs stretch to grasp past
air, talons curl towards
a perching, wings brace, retract,
fold, emptiness below them,
into sustenance and settle.

At ebbing, the abandoned pier reveals
turmoil, seven purple starfish
spread-eagled against the creosote,
barnacles, mussel-clusters,
clutching like 4-year-olds
in front of strangers, touch and cold
exposure straining them, the seize
of sun, the lap of stippled ocean.

Tugboats tread the water, barges
tagging, little brothers in the late
& still shadow, lucent, nudging
aside the midges, shimmered blur
swarming the middle distance. Gull.
Tern. Hawk. Raven. Stars.

CAROUSEL

On the Arrivals Level
a disembodied voice blurs its welcome
FLIGHTS   112   224   CANADIAN   DELTA
mix in static   the fairground chute
the trolley rides   the kiddiecar conveyor belt
a tired diorama

Signs everywhere warn
KEEP HANDS CLEAR   CHECK YOUR LABELS
BAGGAGE MAY LOOK THE SAME   Port
to port the flotsam follows   Sydney
Seattle Tokyo Rome   sisal
passengers with package tape & string
matched plastic & leather trim

Like DNA these spirals   the casual
suited   overdressed
all snatching at the gene pool
mine, there   mine   nabbing or missing
the circling change-of-socks & souvenirs
folded in promise & dismay

Beyond the turnstile   calico observers
smile & smile   holding names
& brass rings   waving & waving
as though to generate the world

III.   Garden Bed

III. Garden Bed

December

skater   on the pond's first ice
   trusting

each stroke a sickle revelation
eyes lips hands hair all alert to motion
   echo
   breath

surface   sliding surface
   erasing space &
   generating distance

     at the heart
         the DANGER sign's posted
     at land's edge   hellebore

        the skater   circling
      stumbles flails   recovers
   reaches past lurch   for a steady arm
    retrieving tuque   & then laughter

JANUARY

aureoled in eyelight
night sky stroking the hills in snow

frost in flower

fern heaven

FEBRUARY

discovers the glass ambiguity of absolutes:
    extent for instance
               telling infinity in seconds
       the instant of reach
      already the point of retreat
         edge marked in moraine

outside   under the overhang
   cold withers the cornstalk
   heat melts the icicle
   earth learns the simple bliss of repetition

MARCH

behind the bandshell
before the sousaphones pump up another
      chorus
damp grass tangles into a blanket

& early daisies   limning the lip of spring
     blink   *She loves you, yeah*
        to the morning star

APRIL

Rain
    drenches hillstone
        down to the vein
    pelts root and crevice
    draws jonquils out of the dark
Rain
    leans like silk
    drifts valleyfold and hayfield
        undulate in seedbed
    skin upon skin

May

suddenly   the stroke of noon perhaps
        sunshine
      radiates   like crimson from slow hawthorn
    heat washing by degrees across trunk & limbs
      qigong
nearness generating bloom
      perfume

count the rings   proximity
      is time's monogram   spelling
        touch
    slowly   through
hunger   tongue   permission

the margins move

air & earth   swim in incandescence
    hearts   elastic as seedlings
          springing alive
    embrace
      perfectly   in lilac
   & rhododendron

JUNE

butterflies
            kiss the rosebush like
eyelashes
            touching there &
there
      breast thigh
bellymound
            bud stem &
flower

        cas-
              cading
                    colour

petals
      ride the senses up &
groundwards

            scent
                  lingering

musk
      hanging like
                    summer
lace
      iris air &
wings

JULY

thyme clutches the ridgeback
         lightly   like Miller
         with clarinet
                  in the mood
              tu va trop vite

wild thyme
         clasps the ridgeback
         counts each stone each
    curved bone   vertebrae
              warm census
         traces step by step
              tu va trop fort

              the hill the hollow
                  rise &   crest of
                                   breathing

thyme
         cups the warm ridgeback
         caresses in the wild
              song's abandon
              in the mood
              summer's sense & now
                                   solace

         breathing gently out
              tu dort

AUGUST

tassels   the colour of

   satin   reach out

      tendrils

   wrapping   in touch

field   wanderers

   cornsilk   kisses

        the air

   the shadow kiss of

5 o'clock   thistle

   answers   earth

         ripens

   twining   helix

cell by   cell

September

following the earth's curve
        downward
sun dipping towards Capricorn
geese V south
      etch geometry into the sky

in the underbrush
basking before the darkness falls
    soapallalie ripens white
    sumac deckles red
    salal shines   still
    green

October

fog lingers
     early mornings
   hugs the ground
      each finger of grass
     longingly
   licks daisy petal patch of clover

    leaving

       no   not yet

    still touching there
      & there

       day
    breaking earthbound body
      into singing

November

garden bed's embrace

last leaves on the vine maple

arms   hands   fingertips

IV. Taking Turns

LOT

Now the city's had its facelift, Lot
won't go back to Whiterock; he can't abide
the artificial fronts, the tea shoppes &
sushi bars & plaster souvenirs
that took the place of clapboard & plain food-
stalls & the slow walk out along
the pier.
              The erratic white rock doesn't
look so big now either, diesel's replaced
the steam train, salmon no longer spawn
in the Campbell: the old romance has gone.
                                              There's more
spice of course on the U.S. side of Boundary
Bay, where skin flickers in oily light
all night long & every day.
                                    But Lot
turns away, sets his jaw, looks north
for the lodestar, & roams the crescent edge
of another part of the ocean, aimlessly grieving.

Amos

Amos works the farm just up
from the Steveston dunes. The dike holds back
the river there, & the tide, & city tourists
come out to hike in long socks and Mountain
Co-op gear, or fondle where they think
they won't be seen.
                        Or both.
                                    Amos sees
more than they guess, harrowing the pumpkin field
& pouring swill.
                        And he accepts more.

He's seen three generations already,
& another wouldn't surprise him, God willing.
He hasn't forgotten being young & wanting
peace, love, the world; the shock is finding it.

Some of the newest neighbours want suburban
fences, want him to sell so they won't have to
smell the barn. Amos figures they'll learn,
so long as they live enough to start remembering.

JOSEPH

Joseph negotiates.
                    It's not that many
people use Iona Beach, being
where it is, by the Treatment Plant
on the River. But always somebody's claiming space
& privilege—so in he steps, outlining
truth & consequences, just like
the game show.
                    Maybe he learned his skills
dockside—or maybe at home: Lord knows
you need survival skills in a big family,
& his *was* big.
                    But he's always been colourful,
& people like him 'cause he speaks their language—
down-to-earth, & generous too, give you
the coat off his back if he thought you needed it,
playing at nothing, & nothing to hide: a grass
roots politician with an honest trade.
Not many like him any more.

Esau

On Wreck Beach, the ones who stand out
are the gazers—teens skipping school
to ogle oiled ingenues, & over-
dressed objectors with pamphlets & sensible shoes—

The drifters, & leatherette habitués
who make it home just go about their lives—
the convention is: *See but don't stare*—

Which makes it all the more remarkable
that everyone, clambering down the ladder, shouldering
knapsack & sleeping mat, noticed the twins—
old Esau & his brother, one shag
& one linoleum—& knew, stripped back
to birthday, they weren't identical:

                              it touched them
how Esau seemed wordlessly to know
when his brother was close to stumbling, & reached out
to steady him, & lead him into shade.

Nimrod

They called him Nimrod,
        the students who followed the north
trail to University Beach (they ate
lunch there on warm spring days,
tossed frisbees & played hackeysack
till psych & physics drew them back up
the cliff), found a name for him just
so he wouldn't seem so threatening—

                                eyes
trained inward, he'd climb the old Martello
towers, scrawled now in claims of hate,
love, & leverage he didn't appear to notice,
& hunt the ghost horizon for signs of war—

not that he ever challenged them, directly,
he just stood apart as though they
& their laughter didn't exist yet, sub-
marines still threatened, & blackouts shaved
the line away that sundered sky from sea.

METHUSELAH

Methuselah jogs to the end of Extension Beach
& back, once, twice, three times, stops,
inhales, flexes his biceps, confirms he's still
alive and hanging loose, & then exhales
& does it again.
                    Hard to know if he lives
in this universe or one of his own
composing.
                    Striding through time, meter
by athletic meter, he stretches rhythm
into private epic: tracks endorphins,
boxes counterclockwise, kicking into
the wind.
                    Clouds scud across the spring
sky, & bold sun-bathers lounge
already topless in leeward hollows.
                                        He's not
immune to nature, but he's piqued by cold
flesh no more than he is by bronzing baby shoes.
Simple: the rime of the ancient: memorabilia.

JEREMIAH

Every morning Jeremiah walks
the sand at Spanish Banks, drifts barefoot
past the clay pools & mussel beds,
hitches up his pantlegs, wades out
to just where the shelf breaks off
into deep blue, & is happy.
                              Overhead,
seagulls swim the wind; & underfoot,
the butter clams bubble down to wakefulness:
the whole world recedes, returns—
                              & in this place,
here, Jeremiah rests.
                    Somewhere
he's found sunshine, so fog sleet
rain do not depress him, they ornament
the air instead, with stipple, the point of living
here being to celebrate touch:

skin, eye, mind, the undulating
purl of intertide, the brindled green.

SAMSON

The cops & social workers put Samson
in a category before he turned 13: *j.d.,*
mostly on property counts—breaking windows,
pulling out fenceposts, smearing graffiti
on office walls—there was arson, too, though never
proved, & an 'incident' with a rival gang.

They tried to reform him, then to lock him away:
by the time he was 23 nothing would hold him,
& then he just disappeared off the edge
of the earth.
                    De-lighted, they joked (peace
treaty sour before it was signed)—

                                        Thirty,
forty years later, he showed up again,
ranging Locarno Beach, haranguing sun
worshippers with Armageddon placards—
THE PIT AWAITS, THE END IS NIGH—& thunder.

JOSHUA

Joshua limps along Jericho Beach
just when the morning tide begins to turn
& the slip of wet sand abandons
bottles & pop cans.
                              Back bent, already
close to the ground, he gathers debris for the few
cents it brings in, enough for a hot
meal, a nearly clean place to bunk
down, & maybe a pack of the makings.
                                                    Sometimes
he sits on one of the logs the Park Board's
chained in rows, watches grain boats
& cruise liners pull out of port, & rolls
a cigarette to ease them off the edge of the world.

In his ears Louis still plays
the blues, *sweet heaven the way the notes*
tumble, & no-one to hear, except himself,
& a coughing fit of mercenary crows.

GIDEON

Gideon camps overnight on Bayswater
Beach, he won't stay at hotels any
more, not since he got thrown out
for rowdiness.
                He still disputes that charge,
insists they mistook his intent: he just needs
to hear the trumpet strut confidence by day,
wind ribbons of loneliness into the night
sky.
       Bayswater's not exactly isolated,
mind, & some of the neighbours call like con-
cierges to have him stopped.
                 Others, listeners,
draw to their open windows in the dark,
& wonder: no lamplight approximates
roadside—
         Gideon alone holds to the land,
until the horn reaches out to the riffing
sea a signature of stars, & the raw
breath of the strait catches the throat in weeping.

GOLIATH

All he ever wanted was to play
beach volleyball at Kitsilano
& then—maybe—Olympics—he had the height—
grew at 12, Goliath—but that's when
the troubles began—they called him *Legs Stretch*
The Giant—tormented him with weather jokes—
The View from Outer Space—you know the kind—
the *un*kind—& then shoved him out
front for every jumped-up rabbiter to take
a potshot at—what they thought
they were doing *I* don't know—all
I know is now he can't co-ordinate
his limbs—lives in a stunted box—watches
a different kind of crowd applauding titans
in bikinis, muttering *Spike, Spike*—

MICAH

While the West End rides at anchor across the bay,
dragons dance point: everyone at Vanier Park
watches the air, balsa boxes pirouette &
clumsy newspaper diamonds leap with ribbon tail
perfect triple salchows in gentian blue.

Micah's the kite-master here: he splits
planes, trains the wind, teaches magic,
plays the guys that hold the ice- and earth-bound
down: he cleaves chartered bureaucrats
from calculated coils, loosens
captains from buttons & generals from polished stars,
till all are poets, children, blind visionaries:

as one they stretch, lift high on tiptoe,
reach for the quickening sky, the arcs, the tangents
liberating strings, shimmer into shining.

JEROBOAM

Straight up—no two ways about it—
Jeroboam drinks.
                    Used
to be he'd march smartly all around
the marketplace, crack jokes at others'
expense, & now-and-then his own—swaggered,
he did, gold chains & flashy rings
& a riding crop he didn't need.
                    Now
he sits on the crusted pilings at the fish dock
on False Creek, next to the swank cafes,
sways back & forth with a brown bag
of cheap wine he sucks on intermittently,
his feet dangling in dried seagull droppings,
& stares vacantly at oil slick & tug.

Local kids show off, jeer, call him
the King of Creosote. They don't see themselves yet.
Nor do the laughing tourists, sipping chardonnay.

JOB

Real estate: that's where Job made his money,
bought a block of the West End just
before land prices skyrocketed
& English Bay was ringed in fantasy

> ... *never a day without problems: con-*
> *tractors, taxes, breaks in the power line,*
> *permits delayed, plumbers on strike, dry-*
> *wallers working roofers' time, rain* ...

> but believing anyway in bumper sticker truths:
> PLANNERS DO IT BY DESIGN, BUILDERS
> NEED DUMPSTERS, NO EXPLOSION WITHOUT
> FIRING: they're posted now in front of churches ...

The Cathedral's still where it was, a few blocks
back of the beachfront, though anyone promenading there
won't see it directly, past the Star
bars, tips, & cappuccino dreams.

ISHMAEL

Hundreds on a summer day skate
or stroll the seawall to Second Beach, swing
in the playground, clamber the monkey bars, or lie
back with a book in the sunshine.
                              Ishmael's one of them
now, having somewhere along the line
come to stilted terms with exile— now
the sand feels like home, the sea an accident
of youth, near enough in memory to shiver
metaphor, but calm enough to bury
nightmare here.
                    Some days he wanders
patriarchally among the caterwauling
children, others he drifts without name
or nametag into story—

                         Telling the days
apart's a privilege of calendars:

for Ishmael, the cataract blur of motion
means above ground, or below.

ABSALOM

It's that same drama that drives him—
being the *next* brother—& nothing anyone
has ever said—*handsome, creative, intelligent,
kind*—dissuades him.
                            So off he storms again,
at night, down the path to Third Beach,
ignoring the Pauline cairn, with the sole intent
of aching back & forth across sand
& seashell, his own private stage.
                                        The steep
slope down angles left, bracken &
Oregon grape clutch at his ankles—his face
blazes, and this time, furrowed, he twists
away & cedar & hemlock branches slap him,
salmonberries snatching from the wings, & he pitches
forward into slugs & stones, distorting the minute
hand & the ground he walks on—
                            Absalom, Absalom,
waiting on morning, & earth upside down—

JONAH

Jonah likes weekdays best at Stanley
Park—smaller crowds—& fewer swimmers
trudge the short path up from Lumberman's
Arch to look at the tropical fish display
in the old aquarium.
                              Jonah cleans there
now, wipes fingerprints off the glass
partitions three, four times a day, more
if school's in, & sweeps lunch litter
through the back doorway, out of sight,
newspapers, candy wrappers, bus
transfers, life.
                        When he's tired, he stops
by the orca pool, leans on the push broom,
& watches the animals watch back, breaching
once, twice, *weren't you the one*, he hears,
weren't you the one, his ears ringing with echoes
he learned at sea, before the nightmares started . . .

HOSEA

Where else but Hallelujah Point
would you expect to find Hosea?
                                    Pacing
the shore, waving dramatically, he belts out
opera every evening—*Nessun dorma,
Di Provenza'il mar, il suol*—whatever
strikes a chord, but mostly Verdi in the blue-green
twilight.
                    The sound billows: ghostly phrases
catch in Lost Lagoon, carry the harbour,
drift on vagrant currents out to sea.

No-one knows his origins: they ask,
but get aria for answer.
                                    The only other
fixture here's the 9-o'clock gun, which volleys
its one-shot long-forgotten curfew
nightly.
                    Every night Hosea, though, breaks off
his singing then, & arms akimbo, bowing
bravo to the cannon, disappears.

ELIJAH

After the first time, when the flames blazed
out of control, rolling as though they had
wheels, Elijah stayed away from weiner
roasts at Sunset Beach: got himself
elected *finally* to Council, badgered the others
till they tired out, gave in,
voted all bonfires unlawful,
& set aside funds to pay patrols.

He's keen on patrols, Elijah, thunders
law-&-order whenever he figures some Jezebel
is up to something—*give 'em one match, they'll ask
for two*, he says, spinning enigmas into
power. An opposition alderman
counsels *charity*, but he mishears, maybe
deliberately, swivels his chair, & fires up
a hot dry sound-bite for the evening news.

SETH

Oh, come on, he says, can't you imagine
what it's been like, going through life
as the Murderer's little brother? First there was no-one
to play with—who'd send their kid to *that*
house, despite the orchard—then school
then work, & some jerk trying
to interrupt the wedding, calling it 'just
cause,' & even now it doesn't matter
where I am—walking Ambleside
with the dog—reporters'll come up & ask
'What was he like?' Always *him, him,*
him, never even Abel, & forget about
me—oh, maybe 'How does it feel?'
Stupid question. How do they *think* it feels?
So long ago, & still like dancing
barefoot on oyster shells, with no pearl.

DANIEL

Daniel's retired now, divides his leisure
time between Dundarave & Lions
Bay, runs this little booth, see,
where he traces yr hand fer love & life lines,
tells yr fortune fer only a dollar, *only*
a dollar folks step right up, ya can hear him
barkin' from up on the highway, ya wouldn' know
he useta run this entire compny, made
breakfast food kamut flakes or one-a them
other old-fashion health fads
that made a mint, read the future right
on that one anyways, who'd of guessed he'd start
sellin' fortune cookies next, with a chain
o' shacks on every beach from here to Squamish,
knows a thing or two, he does, has a heck
of a good life, winters in Maui, readin' the palms.

JEHOSHAPHAT

As soon as the price dropped below some magic
number, the backers pulled out & the copper
mine closed at Britannia Beach. They built
the diving boards after.
                              When fireweed started
to take root in the tailings, they had to act
fast, so dereliction didn't crawl
caterpillar into the people too—
but how to kickstart metamorphosis?
When someone said *tourists*, the platform plans
began: *bingo, casino, golfcourse, bar:*
the usual butterfly sugar.

                              Jehoshaphat
loved the mountains, used to hangglide
when he was young, & figured he'd stopped forever
stroking the air, but when that tower grew out
of the sea, the old man climbed the sky again,
counted to three, & leapt into ultramarine.

SOLOMON

Solomon cuts away from the salt coast,
follows the scimitar divide past
Black Tusk, & inland, riding horseback
in search of calm.
        These days he's plagued
by migraines, the constant clench at his temples as sharp
as propaganda, the lines in his forehead taxed
with deepening recognition. Pressing on
means only pressing on.
        But slowly
sword fern gives way to rhododendron,
& then tiger lily.

        At Alice Lake
he dismounts at last:
            the fresh water beckons—
the apple tree—
        & naked to summer's kiss
he steps off the stone periphery into
the element's embrace, & is sustained.
        Here
is lovesong, drawing him under, & lovesong
is here, comforting, surfacing in light.

ABOUT THE AUTHOR

W.H. New was born in Vancouver and attended UBC and the University of Leeds. Author of four books of poetry and two collections of poetry for children, he is also the general editor of the *Encyclopedia of Literature in Canada*. He has lectured and taught in many countries, including Australia, France, the USA, Finland, China, India, Norway, and New Zealand. Currently he is University Killam Professor at the University of British Columbia.